Andrew Brodie ✓

W0009560

MORE Improving
Comprehension

for ages 5-7

A & C Black • London

Contents

Each text has three comprehension exercises to enable teachers to differentiate across the ability range.

Introduction

Following the success of the Improving Comprehension series, *More Improving Comprehension* provides a further range of interesting and exciting texts for sharing with pupils. The texts have been carefully selected to be appropriate to the age group and to cover a range of text types. The accompanying comprehension worksheets are differentiated at three levels and are designed to be used by individuals or small groups. **Notes for teachers** at the foot of each worksheet provide guidance on how to get the most from the texts and how to approach the questions on the sheet.

For monitoring and recording purposes, an **Individual Record Sheet** is provided on page 4 detailing reading and writing levels appropriate for Years 1 and 2.

How to use the book and CD-ROM together

The book has fifteen texts, which can be projected on to a whiteboard for whole class use from the CD-ROM, or photocopied/printed for use with small groups or individuals. Sharing the text either on screen or paper provides lots of opportunities for speaking and listening, for decoding words through a phonic approach, for reading and re-reading for meaning, and for satisfaction and enjoyment in shared success.

For each text there are three comprehension worksheets at different ability levels to enable teachers to differentiate across the ability range. An animal picture at the top of the sheet indicates the level of the worksheet. The **cat** exercises are at the simplest level; the **dog** exercises are at the next level; the **rabbit** exercises are at the most advanced level. You may decide to give some pupils the cat worksheet and then decide, on the basis of their success, to ask them to complete the dog worksheet. A similar approach could be taken with the dog and rabbit sheets.

After reading the text with the pupils, the teacher should discuss the tasks ensuring that the children understand clearly how to complete the worksheet. Remind them to answer the questions using full sentences and correct punctuation.

National Curriculum levels

The worksheets are aimed at the following ability levels:

Cat worksheets are for pupils working towards Level 1.
Dog worksheets are for pupils working at Level 1.
Rabbit worksheets are for pupils who are working confidently at Level 1 and are progressing towards Level 2.

Individual record sheet

Pupil's name: _____

Date of birth: _____

Reading Level 1

☐ I can recognise familiar words in simple texts.

☐ I can use my knowledge of letters and sound-symbol relationships in order to read words, sometimes with support.

☐ I can use my knowledge of letters and sound-symbol relationships to establish meaning when reading aloud, sometimes with support.

☐ I can express my response to poems, stories and non-fiction by identifying aspects I like.

Reading Level 2

☐ I can show understanding when reading simple texts.

☐ My reading of simple texts is generally accurate.

☐ I can express opinions about major events or ideas in stories, poems and non-fiction.

☐ I can use phonic skills in reading unfamiliar words and establishing meaning.

☐ I can use graphic skills in reading unfamiliar words and establishing meaning.

☐ I can use syntactic skills in reading unfamiliar words and establishing meaning.

☐ I can use contextual skills in reading unfamiliar words and establishing meaning.

Writing Level 1

☐ My writing communicates meaning through simple words and phrases.

☐ I am beginning to show awareness, in my reading or my writing, of how full stops are used.

☐ My letters are clearly shaped.

☐ My letters are correctly orientated.

Writing Level 2

☐ My narrative writing communicates meaning.

☐ My non-narrative writing communicates meaning.

☐ I use appropriate and interesting vocabulary.

☐ I show some awareness of the reader.

☐ I can write a sequence of sentences to show ideas developing.

☐ My sentences are sometimes demarcated by capital letters and full stops.

☐ Usually, I can spell simple, monosyllabic words correctly or spell a phonetically plausible alternative.

☐ My letters are accurately formed.

☐ My letters are consistent in size.

Homes

Meg lives in a flat.

Tariq lives in a bungalow.

Zak lives in a house.

Kim lives in a mobile home.

Homes

Write the correct word under each picture.
Draw your own home.

_____

_____

_____

_____

_____

_____

_____

_____

_____ my home

Word bank

Meg bungalow house Kim flat Tariq mobile home Zak

Notes for teachers

Read the text through with the children, encouraging them to attempt to read it themselves. Talk about each character and their homes. What does each person look like? When you feel that the pupils are confident with the text sheet, give them this worksheet and help them to label the first picture. Can they label the other pictures without help? If you feel that the final box is not big enough, the children could use the back of the sheet for drawing their home.

Homes

Who lives in a bungalow?

_____

_____

Who lives in a mobile home?

_____

_____

Who lives in a flat?

_____

_____

Who lives in a house?

_____

_____

Word bank
Meg Tariq Zak Kim

Notes for teachers
Read the text through with the children, encouraging them to attempt to read it themselves. Talk about each character and their homes. What does each person look like? When you feel that the pupils are confident with the text sheet, give them this worksheet and help them to compose a sentence in response to the first question. Of course, all of the questions could be answered with just the names of the characters but encourage them to write complete sentences.

Homes

Who lives in a mobile home?

_____

_____

What type of home does Meg have?

_____

_____

What type of home does Zak live in?

_____

_____

What type is Tariq's home?

_____

_____

What type of home do you have?

_____

_____

Word bank
bungalow   house   flat   mobile home

Notes for teachers
Read the text through with the children, encouraging them to read it themselves. Talk about each character and their homes. What does each person look like? When you feel that the pupils are confident with the text sheet, give them this worksheet and help them to compose a sentence in response to the first question. Encourage them to write complete sentences for every question. Discuss the pupils' own homes – can they explain whether they live in a house, bungalow, flat, etc? Can they think of any other types of homes?

Peaceful sleep

There's a frog on my hat
And a mouse on my toes.

There's a fly on my ear
And a moth on my nose.

There's a bird on my knee
And some ants in a heap.

There's a cat on my tum
But we're both fast asleep.

Peaceful sleep

Name: _____ Date: _____

Write the words with the pictures.

Word bank
frog   mouse   fly   moth   bird   ants   cat   asleep   hat

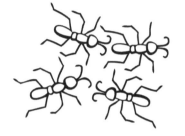

_____   _____   _____

_____   _____   _____

_____   _____   _____

Notes for teachers
Read the poem to the children. If you feel that they are able to do so, help them to read it themselves using their phonic skills to decode any unfamiliar words. Read the instructions with the children then help them to write the words with the pictures. Read through the poem again and encourage the children to read it themselves now that they have practised many of the words that appear in the poem. Ask them to draw one of the animals from the poem on a separate piece of paper.

Peaceful sleep

Who is on the hat?

_____

_____

Who is on the boy's nose?

_____

_____

Who is on the boy's knee?

_____

_____

Which animals are in a heap?

_____

_____

Who is on the boy's tummy?

_____

_____

Notes for teachers

Read the poem through with the children. Encourage them to read it through themselves, using their phonic skills to decode the words – the simple rhymes will help with this process. As with all the passages in this book, the children should listen to you reading the poem several times before they attempt to answer the questions. Ask the children the first question: 'Who is on the hat?' The reply will probably be 'a frog'. Encourage the children to think of a longer answer by repeating the question and then saying 'The frog is …' Practise obtaining a short and long answer with the other questions.

Peaceful sleep

Which animals are on the boy's head?

_____

Which word rhymes with toes? _____

Which word rhymes with heap? _____

Which word is used instead of stomach? _____

Look at the first verse of this rhyme. It is different to the poem.

There's a dog on a lead
And a squirrel in a tree.

Try to write some second lines for each of these verses:

There's a lion on the loose
And _____

There's a bear on my bed
And _____

Choose any animal and write a two-line verse.

_____

_____

Notes for teachers
Read the poem through with the children. Help them to read it themselves by decoding the words using their phonic skills. Look at the rhyme structure with the children, encouraging them to notice that the rhyming words appear at the end of each verse. Discuss ideas for their own lines for the part verses given. They could share their favourite one with the rest of the class.

A butterfly

Here is a butterfly egg.

A caterpillar grows in the egg.

The caterpillar eats lots of leaves.

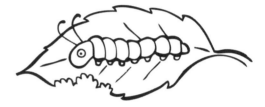

The caterpillar grows bigger.

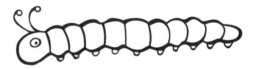

The caterpillar makes a house called a cocoon.

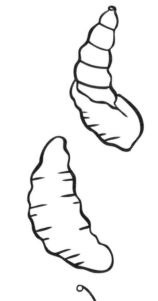

The cocoon hangs on a leaf.

After a few weeks a butterfly comes out of the cocoon.

Name: _____ Date: _____

A butterfly

Use words from the word bank to write a label under each picture.

Word bank
egg caterpillar cocoon leaves leaf butterfly

_____ _____ _____

What does the caterpillar eat?

The caterpillar eats _____

What comes out of the cocoon?

A _____ comes out of the cocoon.

Draw a butterfly.

Notes for teachers
Read and talk about the text with the pupils ensuring that they understand the sequence of events. Once the children are confident with the text, give them this worksheet and discuss what they need to do to complete it. Explain that they won't need all the words that are in the word bank but encourage them to use their phonic skills and their comprehension skills to read each of the words.

  Andrew Brodie: More Improving Comprehension for Ages 5–7 © A&C Black, Bloomsbury Publishing 2012

A butterfly

Write about these pictures.

_____

_____

_____

_____

_____

_____

_____

_____

Have you seen a butterfly?

_____

_____

Notes for teachers
Read and talk about the text with the pupils ensuring that they understand the sequence of events. Once the children are confident with the text, give them this worksheet and discuss what they need to do to complete it. The final question could be answered simply with 'yes' or 'no' but encourage the children to compose a sentence to answer it. If you would like to give the children practice in using phonic skills to segment words for spelling, you could dictate the following: I have seen a butterfly on a flower.

A butterfly

Write about these pictures.

_____

_____

_____

_____

_____

_____

_____

_____

_____

_____

_____

_____

_____

Notes for teachers
Read and talk about the text with the pupils ensuring that they understand the sequence of events. Once the children are confident with the text, give them this worksheet and discuss what they need to do to complete it. As a speaking and listening activity you could talk to the children about caterpillars and butterflies in general, e.g. 'Have you seen a butterfly in the garden?' 'What colour was it?' 'Where was it?'

Fruit and vegetables

Meg's favourite vegetables are carrots.

Tariq's favourite vegetables are peppers.

Zak likes potatoes best of all.

Kim likes peas because they are green.

Meg's favourite fruit is an apple.

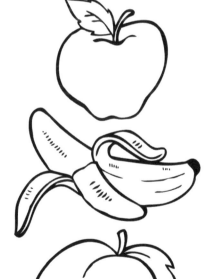

Tariq really likes bananas.

Zak's favourite fruit is a peach.

Kim likes grapes because they are green.

Fruit and vegetables

Write the correct word under each picture.
Draw your favourite fruit.

_____

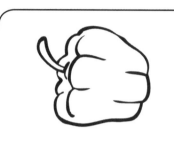

_____

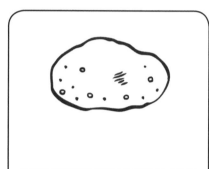

_____

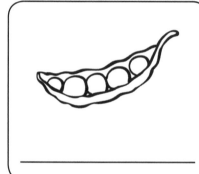

_____

_____

_____

_____

_____

my favourite fruit

Word bank

potato banana carrot apple peas peach pepper grapes

Notes for teachers
Read the text through with the children, encouraging them to attempt to read it themselves. Discuss the word 'favourite', ensuring that each child can say it clearly and can recognise it in the text. Talk about each character and their favourite fruit and vegetables. When you feel that the pupils are confident with the text sheet, give them this worksheet and help them to label the first picture. Can they label the other pictures without help? If you feel that the final box is not big enough, the children could use the back of the sheet for drawing their favourite fruit.

Fruit and vegetables

Who likes carrots best of all?

_____

_____

Who thinks potatoes are his favourite vegetables?

_____

_____

Whose favourite fruit is a banana?

_____

_____

What is your favourite fruit?

_____

_____

What is your favourite vegetable?

_____

_____

Notes for teachers

Read the text through with the children, encouraging them to attempt to read it themselves. Discuss the word 'favourite', ensuring that each child can say it clearly and can recognise it in the text. Talk about each character and their favourite fruit and vegetables. When you feel that the pupils are confident with the text sheet, give them this worksheet and help them to compose a suitable answer for the first question. Can they answer the other questions using complete sentences?

Fruit and vegetables

Who likes peppers and bananas?

_____

_____

Who likes potatoes and peaches?

_____

_____

Who likes peas and grapes?

_____

_____

Why does she like peas and grapes?

_____

_____

What is your favourite fruit? Can you explain why you like it?

_____

_____

Notes for teachers

Read the text through with the children, encouraging them to attempt to read it themselves. Discuss the word 'favourite', ensuring that each child can say it clearly and can recognise it in the text. Talk about each character and their favourite fruit and vegetables. When you feel that the pupils are confident with the text sheet, give them this worksheet and help them to compose a suitable answer for the first question. Can they answer the other questions using complete sentences? The children may need some extra help with the very last question – talking about it first will be very useful. What is it about a particular fruit that makes it their favourite? Is it just the taste or is it the colour, the texture, the skin, etc?

Cat rescue

Jasmin was playing in the garden with her mum and her cat called Cat.

Cat saw a bird in a tree.

Cat began to climb the tree.

The bird flew away but Cat still climbed the tree.

The cat climbed higher and higher.

'Come down, Cat,' said Jasmin.

'Come down, Cat,' said Mum.

'Meeow!' said Cat.

'Cat is stuck up the tree,' said Jasmin.

Mum went to fetch a ladder.

Mum began to climb the ladder.

'Be careful, Mum!' said Jasmin.

Mum was careful. She held on tightly and she picked up Cat.

Jasmin gave her cat a hug.

Cat jumped down. She saw a bird in another tree!

Cat rescue

Who were playing in the garden?

_____, _____ and _____ were

playing in the garden.

Ring the correct word under each picture.

tree   cat   mum

cat   ladder   bird

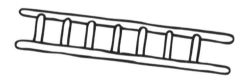

ladder   tree   sky

boy   girl   cat

What do you like to do in the garden?

Notes for teachers

Discuss each of the questions with pupils before they attempt their answers. For the first question, if any children are likely to have difficulty in writing words in the answer spaces let them dictate the answer for you to write in. You may wish to write very lightly for pupils to go over your correctly formed letters.

The final question may be used for discussion only or you may ask children to draw what they like to do in the garden.

Cat rescue

Name: _____ Date: _____

What did the cat do? Put a ring round the correct answer.

Cat played
with a ball.

Cat drank
some milk.

Cat climbed
a tree.

Write the correct word under each picture. Choose words from the box below.

tree bird cat ladder

 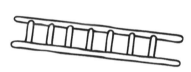 

_____ _____ _____ _____

What do you like to play in the garden?

_____

Notes for teachers
Discuss each of the questions with pupils before they attempt their answers. The first question asks children to choose the correct answer. There are clear picture clues here, so it is important to ensure the children also read the phrases given. The final question allows pupils the freedom to draw and write about activities they would enjoy in the garden.

Cat rescue

Name: _____ Date: _____

Who was playing in the garden?

_____

_____

What did the cat do?

_____

_____

Label each picture. Use the story to help you.

_____ _____ _____

What might the cat do next?

_____

_____

What do you like to do in the garden?

_____

_____

Notes for teachers

Discuss the use of speech marks in the text and ask why there are none in the speech bubble even though the cat's word is written there.

Encourage pupils to write a simple sentence to answer each of the first two questions, using capital letters for the names and a full stop at the end. When answering the second question encourage pupils to look at the text to establish the key point that the cat climbed the tree.

The final two questions could have a variety of answers but what we are looking for is appropriate interpretation of the questions rather than of the text.

 Andrew Brodie: More Improving Comprehension for Ages 5–7 © A&C Black, Bloomsbury Publishing 2012

Car trouble

Mum was driving the car on the motorway.

Suddenly the engine stopped.

There was lots of smoke.

Mum drove the car on to the hard shoulder.

Mum and Joe got out of the car carefully.

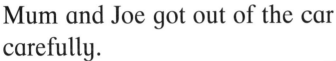

They waited on the grass.

A fire engine came.

A police car came.

The police lady gave Mum and Joe some shiny blankets to keep them warm.

A pick-up truck came.

The car was put on to the pick-up truck.

Mum and Joe got in the truck.

They took the car to be mended.

It cost a lot of money!

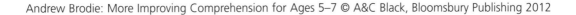

Car trouble

Write the words with the pictures.

Word bank
car
Mum
motorway
smoke

_____

_____

_____

_____

Who was driving the car?

_____ was driving the car.

Who was with Mum in the car?

_____ was with Mum in the car.

Draw a picture of a vehicle on the back of this sheet.

Notes for teachers

Read the text with the pupils, ensuring that they understand the sequence of events – you may like to cut the text into several pieces then ask the pupils to put them in the correct order.

Discuss each of the questions with pupils before they attempt their answers.

The final question may be used as a focus for discussion: Do the children know the word 'vehicle'? What vehicles can the children think of? They may suggest the fire engine, the police car and the pick-up truck from the story.

As an extension activity you could ask the children if they have any of their own experiences of car trouble. What happened?

 Andrew Brodie: More Improving Comprehension for Ages 5–7 © A&C Black, Bloomsbury Publishing 2012

Name: _____ Date: _____

Car trouble

Answer the questions. You might need some of the words in the word bank at the bottom of this sheet.

Who was travelling in the car?

_____

What happened to the car engine?

_____

What did Mum and Joe do?

_____

Choose a word from the word bank to label each picture.

_____ _____ _____

Word bank

Mum   pick-up truck   Joe   car   fire engine   police car

Notes for teachers

Read the text with the pupils, ensuring that they understand the sequence of events – you may like to cut the text into several pieces then ask the pupils to put them in the correct order.

Discuss each of the questions with pupils before they attempt their answers.

As an extension activity you could ask the children if they have any of their own experiences of car trouble. What happened?

Car trouble

Answer the questions.

What type of road were Mum and Joe travelling on?

_____

_____

Why did Mum drive on to the hard shoulder?

_____

_____

Why did Mum and Joe wait on the grass?

_____

_____

Write about a journey you have made.

_____

_____

_____

_____

_____

Notes for teachers
Read the text with the pupils, ensuring that they understand the sequence of events – you may like to cut the text into several pieces then ask the pupils to put them in the correct order.
Discuss each of the questions with pupils before they attempt their answers.
The final question requires the pupils to think about a journey of their own. This could be by any form of transport.
Encourage them to think of an occasion when something unusual happened on the journey.

Firework night

The firework went high,
High in the sky.

The sparks were so bright,
In the dark of the night.

The wind was so cold,
For young and for old.

We warmed by the fire,
As the flames reached up higher.

We went off to bed,
With stars in our heads.

Firework night

Write the second line for each verse.

The firework went high,

_____

The wind was so cold,

_____

Answer the question. Use the words in the word bank.

How did the people keep warm?

_____

_____

Word bank
standing
fire
people
the
warm
by
kept
the

Draw a picture of a star.

Notes for teachers
Read the poem to the children. If you feel that they are able to do so, help them to read it themselves using their phonic skills to decode any unfamiliar words. Encourage one or two children to 'perform' the poem. When the children are confident with the text, give them this worksheet and ensure that they understand the tasks. The first task simply requires the children to use their best handwriting to complete the second lines of two of the verses. The second task is more difficult as the children will need to think about the answer then compose a sentence to express it.

Firework night

Where did the first firework go?

_____

_____

What brightened up the darkness of the night?

_____

_____

Which people felt cold?

_____

_____

Have you been to a firework party?

_____

_____

Word bank
rocket   firework   bonfire   sparks   grandparents   children

Notes for teachers
Read the poem to the children. If you feel that they are able to do so, help them to read it themselves using their phonic skills to decode any unfamiliar words. Encourage one or two children to 'perform' the poem. When the children are confident with the text, give them this worksheet and ensure that they understand the tasks. Note that the final question could simply be answered 'yes' or 'no' – help the children to think about a time when they have seen fireworks and to write a sentence about the occasion.

Firework night

What type of firework was the first verse describing?

_____

_____

What made some people feel cold?

_____

_____

How did they get warm?

_____

_____

Did they really have stars in their heads?

_____

_____

Write about a firework party.

_____

_____

Word bank
rocket firework bonfire sparks grandparents children

Notes for teachers
Read the poem to the children. Help the children to read it themselves using their phonic skills to decode any unfamiliar words. Encourage one or two children to 'perform' the poem. When the children are confident with the text, give them this worksheet and ensure that they understand the tasks. The final question could simply result in a single word answer but help the children to compose an appropriate sentence to answer it.

Hello Jenny

Jenny came in from school.
"Hello Jenny," said the parrot.

Mum came in from work.
"Hello Jenny," said the parrot.
"Silly parrot!" said Mum.

Dad came in from work.
"Hello Jenny," said the parrot.
"I'm not Jenny, I'm Dad," said Dad,
just like he did every evening.

Mum, Dad and Jenny went out.

A cat came in through the window.
"Hello Jenny," said the parrot.
"MEEOW!" said the cat and he
ran away.

MEEOW!

Hello Jenny

Who came in from school?

_____

_____

Who came in from work first?

_____

_____

Who came in through the window?

_____

_____

Who spoke to everyone who came in?

_____

_____

Word bank
Dad cat came parrot Mum Jenny in work school window

Notes for teachers
Read the text with the pupils ensuring that they understand the sequence of events.
Discuss each of the questions with pupils before they attempt their answers. Point out that most of the words that they
will need are contained in the word bank. Encourage each child to read the words out loud.

Hello Jenny

Jenny came in. Where had she been?

_____

_____

Where had Mum and Dad been?

_____

_____

What did the parrot say to everyone who came in?

_____

_____

What happened after Mum, Dad and Jenny went out?

_____

_____

_____

_____

_____

Notes for teachers
Read the text with the pupils ensuring that they understand the sequence of events.
Discuss each of the questions with pupils before they attempt their answers. The final question may have a longer
answer than the previous questions as the children may choose to write about everything that happened rather than
just about the cat coming in. Ask them to think why the cat ran away.

Hello Jenny

Draw a ring around the correct answer.

The story took place …

in the
morning.

in the middle
of the night.

in the early
evening.

Write sentences to answer these questions.

What did the parrot say to everyone?

_____

_____

_____

What did Dad say every evening?

_____

_____

_____

Why did the cat run away?

_____

_____

_____

Notes for teachers
Read the text with the pupils ensuring that they understand the sequence of events. Do they understand that the people were not surprised by the parrot but that the cat did not expect it to speak?
Discuss each of the questions with pupils before they attempt their answers. They may be able to use some creative vocabulary in answering to the final question.

Zip-wire

Jess played on the zip wire.

"Hold on tight," said Grandad.

"I will," said Jess.

It was fun. Jess laughed a lot.

"My turn," said Grandad.

"Hold on tight," said Jess.

"I will," said Grandad.

It was fun.

Grandad let go of the rope.

He fell off.

"Silly Grandad," said Jess.

"Yes, I was silly," said Grandad.

Zip-wire

Who played on the zip wire first?

_____ played on the zip wire first.

Who told her to hold on tight?

_____ told her to hold on tight.

Who fell off?

_____

_____

_____

Write the word to go with each picture.

_____   _____   _____

Notes for teachers
Read the text with the pupils helping them to understand the sequence of events. When they are confident with the story, give them a copy of this worksheet. Discuss each of the questions with pupils before they attempt their answers. The third question requires them to compose their own sentence. Help them to punctuate this appropriately.

Zip-wire

Who was playing on the zip wire?

_____

_____

Who was laughing?

_____

_____

Why did Grandad fall off?

_____

_____

Do you think Grandad was hurt?

_____

_____

Write about a playground you have visited.

_____

_____

_____

Notes for teachers
Read the text with the pupils helping them to understand the sequence of events. When they are confident with the story, give them a copy of this worksheet. Discuss each of the questions with pupils before they attempt their answers. The final question requires them to compose their own answer, which may consist of more than one sentence. Help them to punctuate the answer appropriately.

Zip-wire

Why did Grandad tell Jess to hold on tightly?

_____

_____

Why was Jess laughing?

_____

_____

What did Grandad do that was silly?

_____

_____

Write about your favourite piece of play equipment.

_____

_____

_____

_____

Notes for teachers
Read the text with the pupils helping them to understand the sequence of events. When they are confident with the story, give them a copy of this worksheet. The final question requires them to compose their own answer, which may consist of more than one sentence. Help them to punctuate the answer appropriately.

Andrew Brodie: More Improving Comprehension for Ages 5–7 © A&C Black, Bloomsbury Publishing 2012

Daily weather

Monday morning's full of rain,
Tuesday comes, it's rain again.
Wednesday there is just a drizzle,

Thursday's weather starts to sizzle.
Friday is now hot, hot, hot!
Saturday, find a shady spot.

But when Sunday comes we can go and play
on the beach, in the waves, and stay all day.

Read the poem about the weather then answer these questions.

What was the weather like on Monday?
Draw a ring around the correct answer.

> sunny   foggy   rainy   snowy

What was the weather like on Wednesday?
Draw a ring around the correct answer.

> snowy   drizzly   foggy   sunny

What was the weather like at the weekend?

_____

_____

What is the weather like today?

_____

_____

Word bank
drizzling raining sunny foggy cloudy cold hot warm
mild freezing boiling

Notes for teachers
Read the poem with the children. They may already be familiar with the rhyme 'Monday's Child', which follows a similar structure. You could ask some children to 'perform' the poem. When the children are confident with the text, give them a copy of this worksheet. Discuss the questions so that the children are clear about what they have to do. Point out that the word bank contains words that may be helpful to them and ensure that they can read the words.

Daily weather

Read the poem about the weather then answer these questions.

What was the weather like on Tuesday?

_____

_____

What was the weather like on Friday?

_____

_____

What does the poem say we can do on Sunday?

_____

_____

What is the weather like today?

_____

_____

_____

Word bank
drizzling raining sunny foggy cloudy cold hot warm
mild freezing boiling

Notes for teachers
Read the poem with the children. They may already be familiar with the rhyme 'Monday's Child', which follows a similar structure. You could ask some children to 'perform' the poem. When the children are confident with the text, give them a copy of this worksheet. Discuss the questions so that the children are clear about what they have to do. Point out that the word bank contains words that may be helpful to them and ensure that they can read the words.

Daily weather

Read the poem about the weather then answer these questions.

Describe how the weather changed during the week.

_____

_____

_____

_____

What begins to happen on Thursday?

_____

_____

Why would we need a shady spot on the Saturday?

_____

_____

What would you choose to do on a nice sunny day?

_____

_____

_____

Notes for teachers
Read the poem with the children. They may already be familiar with the rhyme 'Monday's Child', which follows a similar structure. You could ask some children to 'perform' the poem. When the children are confident with the text, give them a copy of this worksheet. The questions on this sheet are particularly difficult as the children will need to interpret the words of the poem.

Deer in the road
Look into our lights,
Then up through the hedge
They leap in their fright.

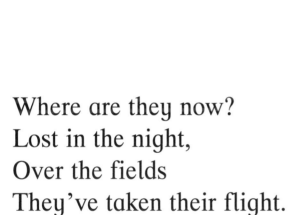

Where are they now?
Lost in the night,
Over the fields
They've taken their flight.

Name: _____ Date: _____

Deer

Draw a ring around the correct answer.

Where were the deer?

In the woods.   In the hedge.   In the road.

What did the deer do?

They jumped   They jumped   They jumped
over a ditch.   through the hedge.   into the woods.

Where did the deer go in the end?

_____

_____

What wild animals have you seen?

_____

_____

_____

_____

Notes for teachers
Read the poem with the children, ensuring that they understand the sequence of events. Discuss each of the questions on this worksheet with the pupils before they attempt their answers. Do they understand how to answer the first two questions?
Talk about the final question. Have the children seen any wild animals in the countryside or the town? Have they seen any animals in the zoo? They will need some support in writing their answers.

        Andrew Brodie: More Improving Comprehension for Ages 5–7 © A&C Black, Bloomsbury Publishing 2012

Deer

Which four words rhyme in the poem?

_____   _____

_____   _____

Write some more words that rhyme with these words.

_____   _____

_____   _____

Where were the deer at the start of the poem?

_____

_____

Where did they go next?

_____

_____

Where did they go in the end?

_____

_____

Notes for teachers
Read the poem with the children, ensuring that they understand the sequence of events. Discuss each of the questions on this worksheet with the pupils before they attempt their answers. Do they understand the use of the word flight in the poem, ie it is a description of the deer fleeing? Help the children to write complete sentences for their answers, encouraging them to use appropriate punctuation.

Deer

How did the writer see the deer?

_____

_____

Why were the deer frightened?

_____

_____

Does the writer know where the deer have gone?
How can you tell?

_____

_____

Describe a wild animal that you have seen.
What animal was it? Where did you see it?
When did you see it?

_____

_____

_____

_____

_____

Notes for teachers
Read the poem with the children, ensuring that they understand the sequence of events. Discuss each of the questions on this worksheet with the pupils before they attempt their answers. Do they understand the use of the word flight in the poem, ie it is a description of the deer fleeing? Help the children to write complete sentences for their answers, encouraging them to use appropriate punctuation. Do they notice that the third task is a double question and that they need to consider both parts? The final task gives them the opportunity to write freely about an animal that they have seen – the three short questions are designed to give them clues as to what to write but they may well have their own extra ideas.

Just right

"Can I sit in the trolley?" asked Jess.

"No, you are too old for that. You are a big girl now," said Mum.

"Can I have a piggy-back?" asked Will.

"No, you are too old for that. You are a big boy now," said Dad.

"Can I go out on my bike?" asked Jess.

"No, you are too young for that. You are only a little girl," said Mum.

"Can I go to the park on my own?" asked Will.

"No, you are too young for that. You are only a little boy," said Dad.

"Can we go to the park?" asked Jess.

"Can we all go?" asked Will.

"Yes," said Mum.

"You are just the right age for that," said Dad.

Just right

Draw a ring around the correct answer.

Who told Jess that she was a big girl?

       Mum   Dad   Will

Who told Jess that she was a little girl?

       Mum   Dad   Will

What was Jess too old to do?

_____

_____

What was Will too old to do?

_____

_____

What was just right for the whole family?

_____

_____

_____

Notes for teachers
Read the story with the children, encouraging them to notice that the parents are first suggesting the children are too big and then suggesting that they are too little! Does this ever happen in their family? Help them to compose sentences to answer the final three questions. They should say these out loud before attempting to write them down.

Just right

Draw a ring around the correct answer.

What did Jess want to do first?

| have a
piggy-back | go to
the park | sit in the
shopping trolley |

What did Will want to do first?

| have a
piggy-back | go to
the park | go out
on his bike |

What was Jess too young to do?

_____

_____

What was Will too young to do?

_____

_____

What do you think you are too big to do now?

_____

_____

Notes for teachers
Read the story with the children, encouraging them to notice that the parents are first suggesting the children are too big and then suggesting that they are too little! Does this ever happen in their family? Notice that tasks 3 and 4 each refer to the second request that each child made. Help the children to think of some ideas for the final task – are there things they would like to do but adults tell them they can't any more?

Name: _____   Date: _____

Just right

Draw a ring around the correct answer.

What did Jess want to do second?

| have a piggy-back | go to the park | go out on her bike |

What did Will want to do second?

| have a piggy-back | go to the park | go out on his bike |

What was Jess too old to do? Who told her that?

_____

_____

What was Will too old to do? Who told him that?

_____

_____

Do you think you are old enough to go out on your bike on your own?

_____

_____

_____

Notes for teachers
Read the story with the children, encouraging them to notice that the parents are first suggesting the children are too big and then suggesting that they are too little! Does this ever happen in their family? Notice that tasks 3 and 4 each consist of two questions – do the children answer both parts effectively in their writing? Talk about the final question with the children both in terms of the answers they could write but also in consideration of safety and welfare issues.

Diary

Lots of things have happened today.

After breakfast, me and Tris sat on the wall by the front gate. We waited ages then we saw Nana and Grandad's blue car. Grandad tooted the horn lots of times.

Mum made Nana and Grandad a cup of tea. They took a long time to drink it. Me and Tris were getting bored.

At last we said goodbye to Mum and got in Grandad's car. It was a long journey to the safari park.

At the safari park we saw elephants and lions. We drove through a field where there were some giraffes. The giraffes came very close to the car and looked

at us through the window. Me and Tris thought it was very funny.

We went in another part where there were monkeys. They climbed on to the car and pulled the windscreen wipers. Grandad thought the wipers might break but they didn't.

I bought a toy monkey and Tris bought a lion. Nana said the monkey looked just like me and she kept calling it Holly.

Tris went to sleep in the car on the way back but I didn't.

Diary

Draw a ring around the correct answer.

What colour was Nana and Grandad's car?

blue   white   red

What did Nana and Grandad have to drink?

hot chocolate   coffee   tea

Where did the children go with their grandparents?

_____

_____

What animals did they see?

_____

_____

What toys did they buy?

_____

_____

Notes for teachers
Read the story with the children, ensuring that they understand the sequence of events. Talk about days out that the pupils may have experienced themselves: do they go out with their grandparents? Have they ever visited a safari park? Help them to compose sentences orally then encourage them to write the sentences, using appropriate segmentation skills to spell the words.

Diary

Name: _____ Date: _____

Draw a ring around the correct answer.

What were the children waiting for?

Christmas   their parents   their grandparents

Where were the children waiting?

on a wall   on a gate   on a swing

Was the safari park close by?

_____

_____

Which animals climbed on the car?

_____

_____

Write about a day out that you have had.

_____

_____

_____

_____

_____

Notes for teachers
Read the story with the children, ensuring that they understand the sequence of events. Talk about days out that the pupils may have experienced themselves: Do they go out with their grandparents? Have they ever visited a safari park? Help them to compose sentences orally then encourage them to write the sentences, using appropriate segmentation skills to spell the words.

Draw a ring around the correct answer.

What toy did Tris buy?

toy giraffe   toy monkey   toy lion

What toy did the girl in the story buy?

toy elephant   toy monkey   toy lion

What did the children find boring?

_____

_____

What did the children find funny?

_____

_____

What do you think the girl's name was? How do you know this?

_____

_____

On the back of the sheet, write about a day out that you have had.

Notes for teachers
Read the story with the children, ensuring that they understand the sequence of events. Talk about days out that the pupils may have experienced themselves: Do they go out with their grandparents? Have they ever visited a safari park? Help them to compose sentences orally then encourage them to write the sentences, using appropriate segmentation skills to spell the words.

Shops

Read what Jess has written about the shops in her town.

There are lots of shops in my town.

There's a newsagents where you can buy newspapers and magazines. They also sell sweets and ice-creams so I like that shop.

Next door to the newsagents there's a chemist. If anyone in the family is ill we go there to get our medicines.

Across the road there is a supermarket where we get most of our food. It's really boring but I don't often go in there because Mum goes when I'm at school.

Near the supermarket there's a shop that sells clothes and curtains and pet food and garden tools and plastic bowls and just about everything you can think of. I don't like it in there unless Ashley comes with me because then we can play hiding from each other.

I like the bookshop. It's not very big but it's got lots of the books I like and I buy them sometimes.

My town is the best town in the world.

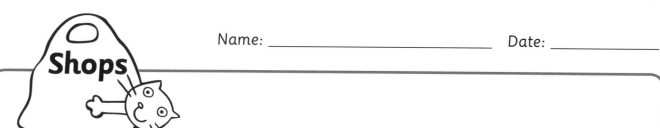

Who is writing about the shops?

_____

_____

What type of shop sells newspapers and magazines?

_____

_____

At which shop do the family get most of their food?

_____

_____

What do the family get from the chemist?

_____

_____

What is the name of your local town?

_____

_____

Notes for teachers
Read the passage with the children, helping them to use their blending skills in reading the tricky words.
Discuss each of the questions with pupils before they attempt their answers. Talk about your own local town and the shops that can be found there – your pupils will probably refer to the shops by name. Can they remember some of the things that each shop sells?

Shops

Which shops does Jess like?

_____

_____

Why does Jess like the newsagents?

_____

_____

What shop is next to the newsagents?

_____

_____

Why doesn't Jess usually go in the supermarket?

_____

_____

Write about one of the shops that you sometimes visit.

_____

_____

_____

_____

_____

Notes for teachers
Read the passage with the children, helping them to use their blending skills in reading the tricky words.
Discuss each of the questions with pupils before they attempt their answers. Talk about your own local town and the shops that can be found there – your pupils will probably refer to the shops by name. Can they remember some of the things that each shop sells? Help them to think of ideas for the final question: Do they like the shop? What does it sell? Where is it? What is it called?

Shops

Why does Jess like the bookshop?

_____

_____

Do you think you would like the bookshop?
Explain why.

_____

_____

Why would Jess's family go to the chemist?

_____

_____

Jess's Mum buys food in the supermarket. Can you
think of other things you could buy in a supermarket?

_____

_____

Write about some of the shops in your town.

_____

_____

_____

_____

_____

Notes for teachers
Read the passage with the children, helping them to use their blending skills in reading the tricky words.
Discuss each of the questions with pupils before they attempt their answers. Talk about your own local town and the
shops that can be found there – your pupils will probably refer to the shops by name. Help them to think of ideas for
the final question: they may like to use the text to give them some clues.

Stormy day

When William woke up, he could hear the wind blowing outside. The trees were waving and millions of leaves were bashing against each other making a loud swishing noise.

William could hear a banging sound so he looked out of the window. The shed door was open. The wind kept knocking it backwards and forwards.

Will got out of bed and got dressed quickly. He opened the back door carefully so that the wind didn't catch hold of it. He closed the door behind him and walked down the path towards the shed. He had to struggle to walk because the wind was so strong.

The shed door was swinging dangerously. When the wind blew and the door closed, Will rushed to the shed and pushed the bolt across.

He turned to go back to the house and saw his mum.

"What are you doing outside, Will?" called Mum. "It's too dangerous in this wind."

"I'm all right!" shouted Will.

Suddenly there was a loud crashing noise. A huge tree came crashing down right across the garden. The path was completely blocked.

Stormy day

Who could hear the wind blowing outside?

_____

_____

What was making a loud swishing noise?

_____

_____

What was making a banging sound?

_____

_____

Why couldn't Will get back to his house?

_____

_____

What is the weather like today?

_____

_____

_____

Notes for teachers
Read the passage through with the children, ensuring that they understand the sequence of events.
Discuss each of the questions with pupils before they attempt their answers. Talk about today's weather. Can the children describe it orally? Help them to compose a sentence that summarises it then encourage them to use their segmenting skills in spelling the words they wish to write.

Stormy day

Why did Will open the back door carefully?

_____

_____

How did Will lock the shed door?

_____

_____

Do you think Will's Mum was cross with him?

_____

_____

What made the loud crashing noise?

_____

_____

Do you remember a time when the weather was very unusual?

_____

_____

_____

_____

Notes for teachers
Read the passage through with the children, ensuring that they understand the sequence of events.
Discuss each of the questions with pupils before they attempt their answers. The final question could result in a simple 'yes' or 'no' answer but encourage the children to describe a particular weather feature that affected their own lives. They could describe a particularly hot or cold day, a very rainy or snowy day, a thunderstorm or a windy day that they have experienced.

Stormy day

Name: _____   Date: _____

Why did Will get dressed quickly?

_____

_____

Why was Will struggling to walk down the path?

_____

_____

How did Will manage to bolt the door safely?

_____

_____

Why did Will have to shout to his Mum?

_____

_____

Describe how you think William would get back to the house.

_____

_____

_____

_____

_____

Notes for teachers
Read the passage through with the children, ensuring that they understand the sequence of events.
Discuss each of the questions with pupils before they attempt their answers. The final question provides the children with an opportunity to write creatively. Encourage them to empathise with Will: how would they feel in his position? What would Mum do? What would Will do? Would anybody else be involved?